Sally can't see

Palle Petersen

The John Day Company   New York

Copyright © 1974 by Palle Petersen. First published in Denmark
by Borgens Forlag A/S
English translation copyright © 1976 by A & C Black Ltd. All rights reserved.
First United States edition 1977. Printed in Great Britain.
0–381–90058–4 (RB)   CIP in the back of the book

Two girls are walking out together
in the sunshine.
Sally's hair is long and dark
and Pat's is short and fair.
Pat isn't as tall as Sally,
though both girls are twelve years old.

Both can hear the birds and smell the flowers,
feel the hot sun on their faces
and the hard path under their feet.
And Pat looks at everything around her.

But Sally can't see.

She is quite used to what we call darkness
because she was born blind.

This is what Sally sees.
We call this color black
and this is what it is like for Sally
whether the sun is shining
or the moon is bright.

Close your eyes tight and cover them with your hands.
Then you will see all that Sally can see.

Because of her blindness Sally goes to a special school.
She doesn't go home at the end of each day.
Instead, she sleeps at school every night
until the end of the term when her mother and dad come
to take her home for the holidays.

It is important for all children
to learn to take care of themselves.
But it is especially so for Sally,
and her teachers help her in all kinds of ways.

Sally knows when the sun is shining—
she can feel its warmth.

But for her there is one sense missing.
Usually we have five senses—
    to see
    to hear
    to feel
    to smell
    to taste.

And Sally can't see.
She can feel the shape and softness of the flowers
and the dustiness of the dry soil
and she can hear the bees buzzing,
so she knows it is a summer's day.

In school, Sally works hard
at finding out the shapes of things,
and she runs her fingers carefully
over every object.
This one is long and thin and cold.
She can feel it has scales,
a pointed mouth, fins, and a tail,
and she knows it is a fish and lives in water.

And Sally learns and remembers with her fingers.

In her twelve years, Sally has learned a lot
about sounds.
The different sounds of people's feet and voices,
the banging of doors
and the clatter of dishes in the sink.

With other children she has a lot of fun
learning about music and the sounds it makes.
The thud, thud, thud of a drum,
the high sweet tones of a recorder
and the tinkle of a tambourine.

And Sally learns and remembers with her ears.

Because Sally couldn't see
it took her a long time to learn to read and write,
but she managed it.
And this is because of Braille writing.

This is a way of making letters with bumps
that you can feel because they stick up on the page.
The bumps make patterns
and Sally has had to learn the patterns with her fingertips
and remember them.

Now Sally reads a lot of Braille books
and enjoys the stories.
But she can't read as fast as her friend Pat.

And she has learned to type
and writes letters home on a typewriter.
But if anyone sends her a letter or a card,
a sighted person has to read it to her.

Here are the shapes used in Braille
for the letters of the alphabet and numbers.

a	b	c	d	e	f	g	h	i	j

k	l	m	n	o	p	q	r	s	t

u	v	w	x	y	z

1	2	3	4	5	6	7	8	9	0

Try using these shapes as a code.

Imagine swimming when you can't see!
But Sally has learned not to be afraid of the water.
And if she knocks into someone,
she laughs and pushes herself away
and swims on.

There is always a grown-up close by
who can watch and help Sally
and the other blind children
if they need it.

When Sally was learning to jump,
she started with the rope close to the ground.
But now the rope is quite high
and she feels for its height with her fingers
before she jumps.
And there is a big pit of soft sand to land on,
which makes Sally feel safe.

And always the teacher is close at hand.

This is Pip, Sally's parakeet.
She has taught him to talk,
and she cleans out his cage every day.

Pip often flies around the room,
then comes to land on Sally's finger
or her head.
They are good friends
and at holiday times
they spend many hours together.

And with her ears and fingers
Sally has learned a lot
about this little bird.

6,955

Instead of having
pictures to look at,
Sally has shapes
to feel.
She has learned
to remember
with her fingertips
and knows a lion
or a number
or even the shape
of a country.

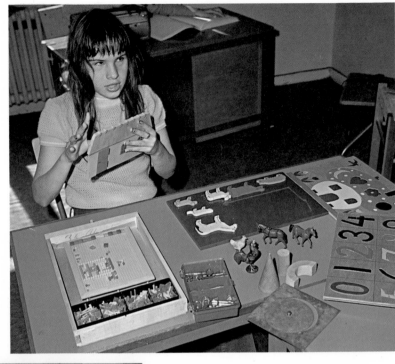

But it takes longer
when you are blind,
and you have to learn
to be patient.

At Sally's school`there is a tape recorder
and she can listen to stories on the headphones.

Sometimes she records stories herself
for other children to listen to.

Best of all, Sally likes the days
when she has riding lessons.
She always has the same horse called Prince
who is gentle and steady.
But a sighted person keeps close at hand
to help Sally to be confident
and sure of herself.

Because of her riding, Sally has learned a great deal
about her horse.
She knows about his shape and size, the feel of his coat,
and how he stands on his four strong legs.

So she has been able to help
to make a model of a horse in the classroom.
Some of the children are not completely blind
and this helps when they are all working together.

When she is at home
for the holidays,
Sally likes to go
shopping on her own.
But she can only go
along the streets
she knows well,
using her long
white cane
to feel the way.

As she steps forward with her right foot,
she swings her cane to the left
because the cane has to feel for the place
where her left foot is going to tread.
This way Sally can be sure there is nothing
to stumble over.
Her white stick shows other people
that she is blind and it helps her to find the curb
or feel for a lamppost or a step.

And all the time, Sally listens.
She can hear the cars,
but she is still afraid of bicycles
because they move so quietly and are so difficult to hear.

At home she knows
just where every bit
of furniture stands.
Her mother is careful
never to put anything,
even a chair,
in a different place.

Sally likes playing
the organ.
She learns the notes
from music written
in Braille,
so she feels the bumps
with her left hand
and plays the tune
with her right.

Nearly every summer
Sally goes to the seaside
with her mother and dad,
and she loves to swim and play in the water.

But sometimes she meets strangers
who are sorry for her
and curious about her blindness.
This makes Sally upset and cross
because these people seem to think
there is something strange about her.
And all she wants is to be treated
as much like other children as possible.

So if ever *you* meet a blind person,
remember Sally
who every day is learning so much,
although she cannot see.